YOU CAN DRAW PLANES, TRAINS, AND OTHER VEHICLES

by Brenda Sexton

PICTURE WINDOW BOOKS
a capstone imprint

MATERIALS

Before you start your amazing drawings, there are a few things you'll need.

pencil

colored pencils

markers

eraser

paper

ruler

SHAPES

Drawing can be easy! In fact, if you can draw these simple letters, numbers, shapes, and lines, YOU CAN DRAW anything in this book.

letters

A B C D
T U W

numbers

1 2 3

shapes

lines

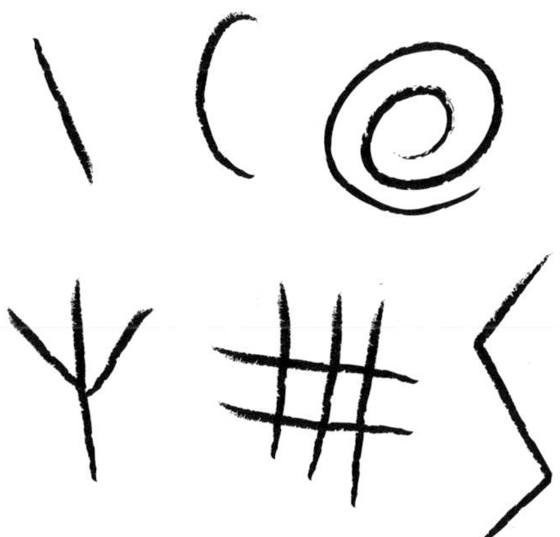

Fire Truck

Speedboat

Submarine

Police Car

Race Car

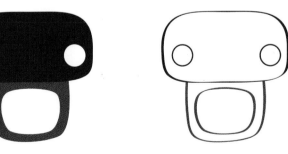

Taxi

Little Red Car

9

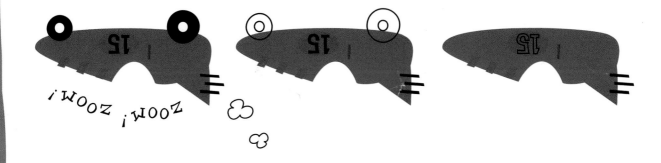

zoom! zoom!

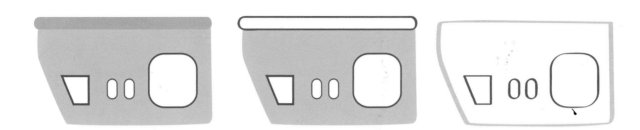

Ice-Cream Truck

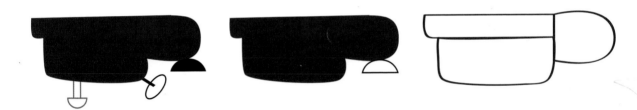

Tractor

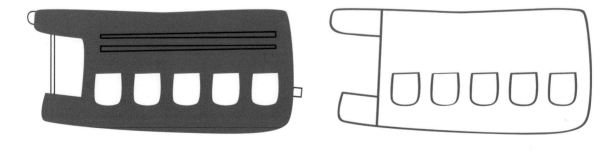

School Bus

Now try this!

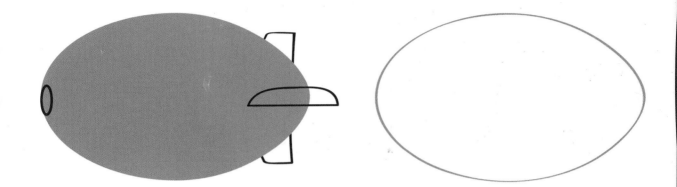

Blimp

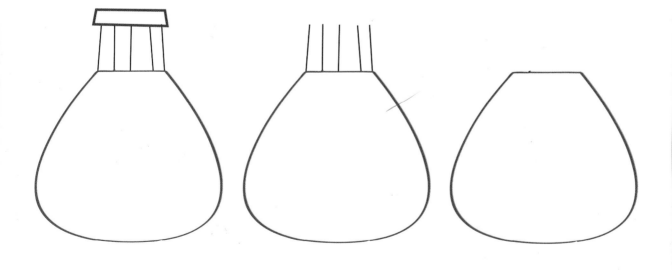

Hot Air Balloon

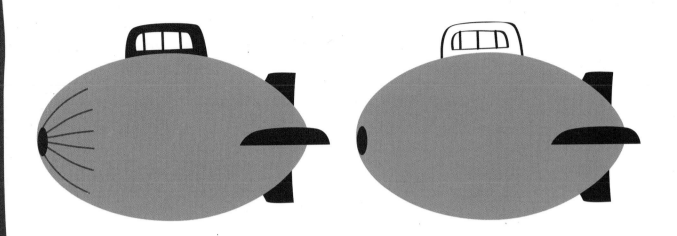

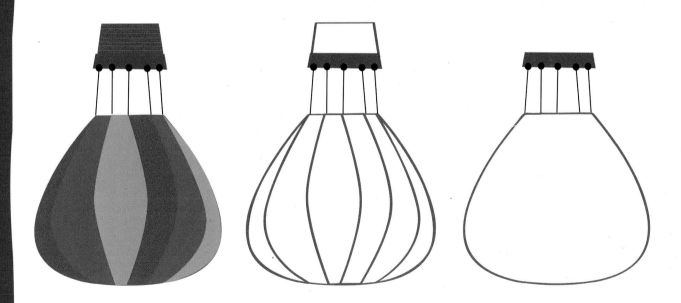

Pickup Truck

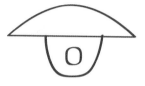

Four-Wheeler

Golf Cart

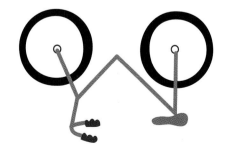
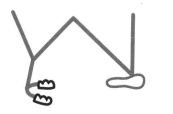

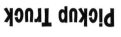

Bicycle

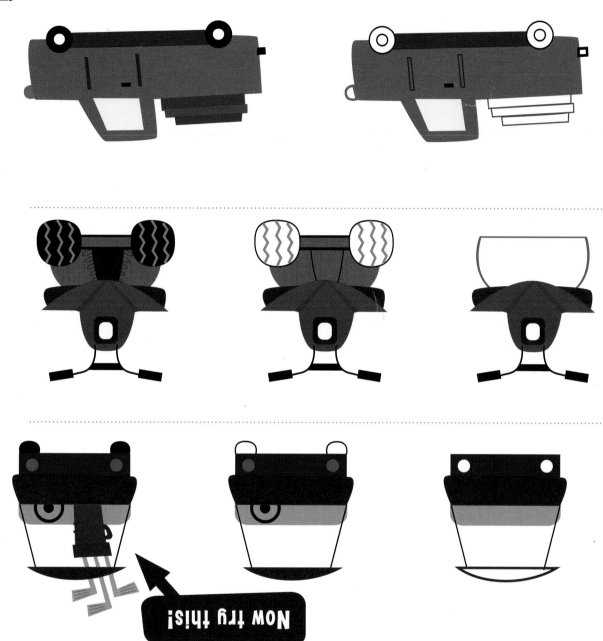

Now try this!

 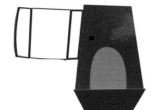 

Train

  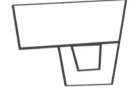

Skid Loader

  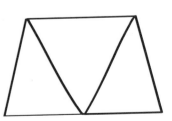

Dump Truck

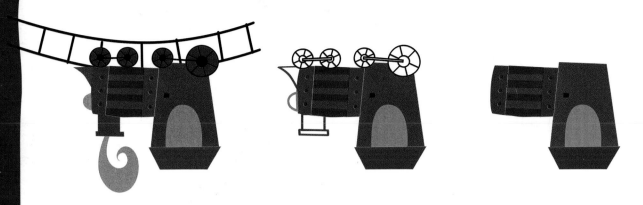

Now try this!

Monster Truck

Helicopter

Rocket Ship

Airplane

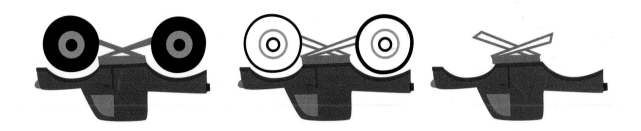

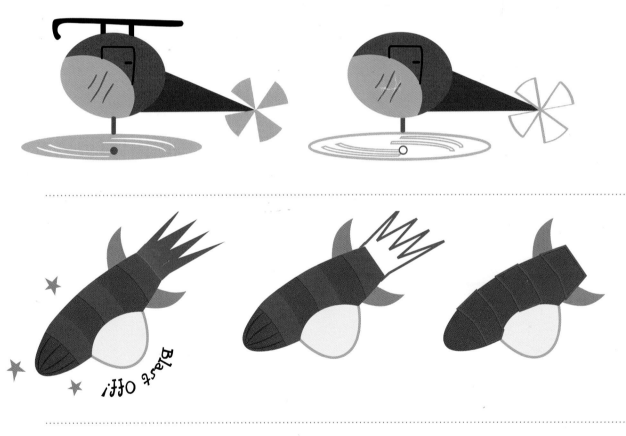

Blast Off!

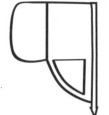

Semitrailer Truck

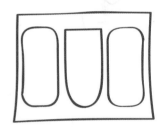

Trolley

Sailboat

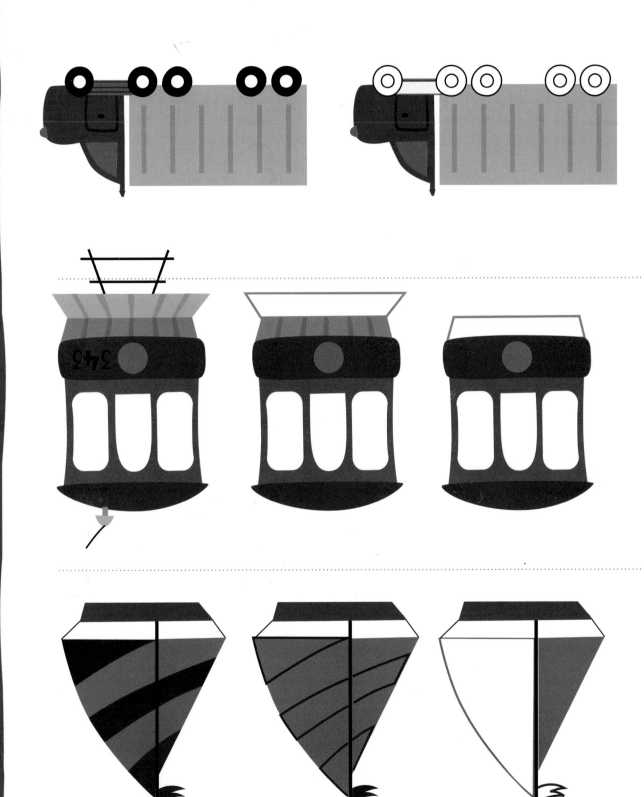

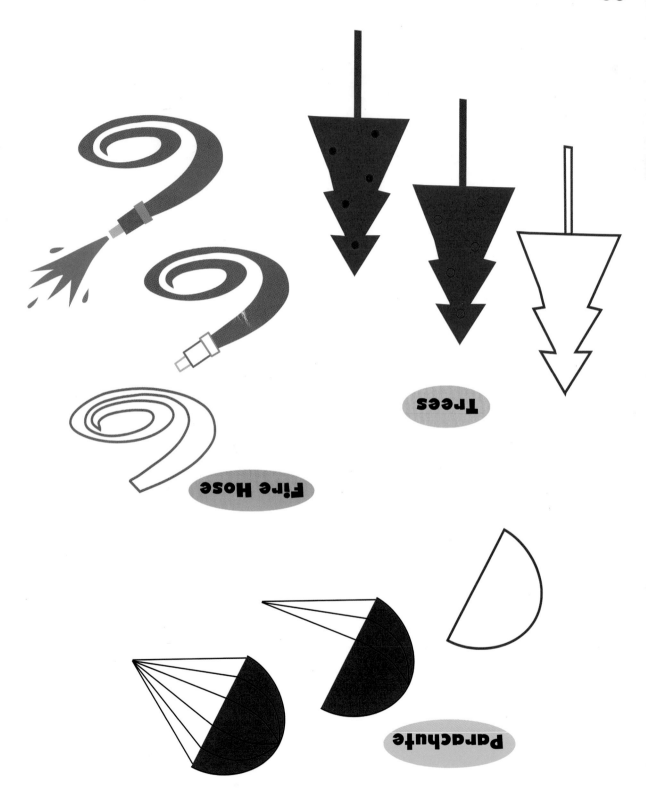

Trees

Fire Hose

Parachute

Ladder

Life Preserver

Waves

Clouds

All books published by Picture Window Books
are manufactured with paper containing at least
10 percent post-consumer waste.

Library of Congress Cataloging-in-Publication Data
Sexton, Brenda.
  You can draw planes, trains, and other vehicles / by Brenda Sexton ;
illustrated by Brenda Sexton.
     p. cm. — (You can draw)
  ISBN 978-1-4048-6278-4 (library binding)
  1. Motor vehicles in art—Juvenile literature.
  2. Drawing—Technique—Juvenile literature. I. Sexton, Brenda. II. Title.
  NC825.M64B78 2011
  743'.89629046—dc22
                              2010030024

Printed in the United States of America in North Mankato, Minnesota.
092010
005933CGS11

Picture Window Books
151 Good Counsel Drive
P.O. Box 669
Mankato, MN 56002-0669
877-845-8392
www.capstonepub.com

Editor: Shelly Lyons
Designer: Matt Bruning
Art Director: Nathan Gassman
Production Specialist: Sarah Bennett
The illustrations in this book were created digitally.

Internet Sites •

FactHound offers a safe, fun way to find Internet sites related to this book.
All of the sites on FactHound have been researched by our staff.

Here's all you do:

Visit *www.facthound.com*

Type in this code: 9781404862784

Check out projects, games and lots more at
www.capstonekids.com

Look for all the books in the **You Can Draw** series:

YOU CAN DRAW
DINOSAURS

YOU CAN DRAW
FLOWERS

YOU CAN DRAW
MONSTERS
AND OTHER
SCARY THINGS

YOU CAN DRAW
PETS

YOU CAN DRAW
PLANES, TRAINS,
AND OTHER VEHICLES

YOU CAN DRAW
ZOO ANIMALS